Fact Finders®

NASTY (BUT USEFUL!) SCIENCE

BAT SPIT, MAGGOTS, and Other Amazing MEDICAL WONDERS

by Kristi Lew

Consultant:
Michael Bentley
Professor of Biology
Minnesota State University, Mankato

CAPSTONE PRESS
a capstone imprint

Fact Finders are published by Capstone Press,
1710 Roe Crest Drive, North Mankato, Minnesota 56003.
www.capstonepub.com

Library of Congress Cataloging-in-Publication Data
Lew, Kristi.
Bat spit, maggots, and other amazing medical wonders / by Kristi Lew.
p. cm.—(Nasty (but useful!) science)
Summary: "Describes some disgusting, but very useful, medical treatments"—Provided by publisher.
Includes bibliographical references and index.
ISBN 978-1-4296-4537-9 (library binding)
ISBN 978-1-4296-6344-1 (paperback)
1. Medicine—Miscellanea—Juvenile literature. I. Title.
R706.L4768 2011
610—dc22
2009050343

Editorial Credits

Jennifer Besel, editor; Matt Bruning, designer; Eric Manske, production specialist

Photo Credits

Alamy: blickwinkel, 9 (leech mouth), Deco Images II, 11 (brain x-ray), Phototake/Scott Bodell, 23, Visuals Unlimited/Dr. David M. Phillips, 11 (blood clot); Capstone Studio: Karon Dubke, 29 (cotton swab); CDC: Janice Carr, 25 (bacteria); Getty Images: Scott Camazine, 13 (wound); Image supplied by Comvita Ltd, 17; iStockphoto: Sebastian Kaulitzki, 25 (digestive system); Science Source: Eye of Science, 13 (maggot close-up), Volker Steger, 14; Shutterstock: Amee Cross, 29 (snake), Andrew Gentry, 5, Cathy Keifer, 29 (snake), D. Copy, 9 (leech), Dmitriy Shironosov, 5 (chicken), Halina Yakushevich, 22, Li Wa, 26, markhiggins, 19, Michael Lynch, 5 (bat), 11 (bat), Mircea Bezergheanu, 5 (leech), 7, newphotoservice, 29 (scientist), Sebastian Kaulitzki, 21 (brain), Sergey Goruppa, cover (maggots)

Printed and bound in China. PO5070

TABLE OF CONTENTS

AMAZING MEDICINE

What do you think of when you hear the word medicine? Probably a bottle of pink liquid. Maybe a doctor's office comes to mind. But would you ever think of fat, wiggling, flesh-eating creatures? How about bee barf or bat spit?

These gross ideas may sound like something from a horror movie. But surprisingly, they are medicines being used today. Medicines like **antibiotics** are doctors' first choice. But modern medical methods don't work on every patient. Sometimes bloodsucking worms are the way to go.

And doctors aren't stopping there. Researchers are looking into ways to use poisonous animals and chicken heads to help people too. These ideas sound weird, but they are saving and improving lives every day.

antibiotic: a drug that kills bacteria

BLOODSUCKING BUDDIES

Hundreds of years ago, doctors used leeches to heal patients. The practice fell out of favor in modern medicine. But today, using leeches to suck a patient's blood is making a comeback. Yes, having a worm suck your blood can be a good thing.

Leeches are worms that drink blood. They usually snack on fish or turtle blood. But they'll suck human blood too. Their hunger for blood isn't nice when you're swimming in a lake. But doctors have found this worm's eating habits very useful.

Normally, your blood flows freely through your body. But sometimes blood clumps up and forms a clot. Clots get stuck in **blood vessels**, stopping the flow of blood. Without blood, **flesh** dies and must be removed. If a blood clot forms in your injured foot, the flesh could die. Then doctors would have no choice but to take off the foot.

medical leeches

But never fear! Leeches to the rescue. The little creepy crawlers can get into places like inside your nose or between your toes. And when they bite down, their powerful spit stops blood from clotting. Turn the page to find out how it works.

blood vessel: a tube that carries blood through your body

flesh: the soft part of a person's body that covers the bones

A leech has a sucker on both ends of its body. The fat end is its rear. The worm uses this sucker to hold on to dinner. The thin end is the animal's head. The mouth sucker has three jaws with hundreds of tiny, needle-sharp teeth.

When a leech sinks its teeth into a juicy blood vessel, its spit seeps into the wound. The leech's spit contains a chemical called hirudin (hi-ROO-din). Hirudin is the ingredient that prevents blood from clotting.

Hirudin prevents a **protein** called fibrin from forming in the blood. If fibrin forms, it makes a web that captures blood cells and forms a clot. As a leech sucks on a patient, its spit prevents fibrin from forming. The leech gets a big supper, and the person's blood doesn't clot. Everyone wins!

FOUL FACT

After feeding, a leech can go six months without another meal. But medical leeches only get one meal. They are destroyed after one use so blood isn't passed around.

protein: a naturally occurring substance in the body

You would think that all this biting and sucking would hurt. But you might not even know if a leech latches onto you. Leech spit has a natural painkiller in it. Leeches might be slimy and nasty, but they're amazing little critters.

mouth sucker

BAT SPIT

Another little creature that likes blood is the vampire bat. The thought of a bat sinking its teeth into flesh is creepy. But bat spit might save lives.

Scientists discovered an **enzyme** in vampire bat spit called DSPA. It turns out that DSPA destroys fibrin in blood. DSPA is different from the chemical in leech spit. Leech spit keeps fibrin from forming. DSPA destroys fibrin that has already formed.

This finding is wonderful news for **stroke** victims. Some strokes are caused by a clot in a blood vessel in the brain. The clot-busting drugs doctors use on patients now can only be used during the first three hours after a stroke occurs. If the drugs are used after that time, they destroy healthy brain tissue.

enzyme: a protein that causes chemical reactions

stroke: a medical condition caused by a sudden lack of oxygen to the brain

USING DSPA ON BLOOD CLOTS

1 Blood clot forms in the brain.

Doctors give stroke patients medicine containing DSPA from bat spit.

2

3 The DSPA breaks up the fibrin, letting blood flow free.

FOUL FACT

A vampire bat will drink about half its weight in blood every night. DSPA stops the prey's blood from clotting so the bat can get its fill.

Many stroke patients don't make it to the hospital in time for current medicines to be effective. But DSPA seems to be safe to use for up to nine hours after the start of a stroke. Doctors are testing DSPA on stroke patients now. One day, vampire bat spit just might save the life of someone you know.

FLESH-EATERS

Have you ever had a cut that took a long time to heal? Some people get sores or wounds that refuse to heal. These injuries don't heal because blood can't get to the **tissues** that need it. Without blood flow, tissue dies. Doctors have to remove dead tissue before it becomes infected.

That's where maggots can help. Maggots look like fat, white worms. But they aren't worms. They are young flies. And maggots are hungry for dead tissue! In a wound, maggots use their fanglike mouth hooks to scrape up dead flesh. As they squirm around, they release enzymes. Enzymes break down dead tissue but don't harm healthy tissue.

The enzymes turn the black, dead flesh into a soup the maggots slurp up. Lucky for patients, maggots are tiny, so the scraping and eating doesn't hurt.

tissue: a mass of cells that form a certain part or organ of a person

maggots

mouth hooks

RAISING MAGGOTS

Doctors don't use maggots that have grown on trash heaps. They use specially raised medical maggots. These maggots come from captive flies that lay their eggs on bacteria-free liver. Scientists carefully clean the eggs to make sure they don't have any **microorganisms** on them. Then the eggs are left to hatch in a bacteria-free environment. Only maggots raised this way are clean enough to put on people's wounds.

microorganism: a tiny living creature that can't be seen without a microscope

Sometimes a wound gets infected. Infections are caused by microorganisms. If microorganisms called bacteria get into a wound, they can cause flesh to rot. Rotting flesh doesn't just turn black. It oozes a smelly liquid. If doctors can't get rid of the bacteria, the person could die. Doctors usually use antibiotics to kill bacteria. But sometimes antibiotics don't work. Don't worry! Doctors put maggots to work eating the bacteria and cleaning the wound.

To most people, having squirming worms inside their open wound sounds horrible. But after the maggots have done their job, the wound is nice and clean. And healthy tissue can grow back.

FOUL FACT

Maggots dine on someone's flesh for 48 to 72 hours. During that time, they grow nearly five times bigger.

BEE BARF

If maggots aren't around to slurp up bacteria, doctors can use honey. That sounds good until you learn that honey is actually bee barf.

Bees go out and gather nectar, a sweet liquid made by flowers. The nectar mixes with enzymes inside the bees' bodies. Then the bees puke the mixture into the hive. Other bees then chew on the nectar mixture before spitting it into the honeycomb. In time, the bee vomit thickens. Presto-chango, you've got some tasty bee barf to spread on your toast. Or, if you're a doctor, to spread on a patient's wound.

Honey is a natural antibiotic. Doctors have found that a particular type, called manuka honey, has very strong antibiotic properties. Manuka honey only comes from New Zealand and Australia. Bees there gather nectar from manuka bushes, which give the honey its unique qualities.

One of the most serious infections today is caused by a bacteria known as MRSA. This bacteria can't be killed by most medical drugs. But manuka honey can kill it. Doctors place bandages covered in the honey on the wound. The honey takes care of the rest. And it doesn't cause side effects like other antibiotics. Pass the bee barf, and save a life!

manuka honey bandage

VITAL VENOM

Many people suffer from high **blood pressure**. The condition is caused by a chemical in the body called angiotensin II (an-je-oh-TEN-sen TWO). This chemical makes muscles around blood vessels tighten. The narrowing vessels make the heart work harder, causing blood pressure to go up. But by studying snake venom, doctors discovered a way to keep those tubes open.

In Brazil, farmers collapsed after being bitten by Brazilian pit vipers. They would fall because the bites caused their blood pressure to drop suddenly. Unfortunately, the snake's venom caused such a huge drop in blood pressure that it killed them too.

Scientists studied the venom. They found a protein in the venom that stops the body from making angiotensin II. Scientists created the protein in the laboratory. Now there are drugs that safely lower blood pressure in people. All thanks to the poisonous pit viper!

blood pressure: the force of blood as it flows through the body

MILKING SNAKES

Snake venom can be deadly. But as with the Brazilian pit viper, it can also be helpful. To know what could be useful, scientists have to study the venom. That means they have to get the venom. Scientists milk snakes to collect their poison. This can be a dangerous job! The scientist must get a snake to bite a flexible covering attached to a container. When the snake bites, venom squeezes out of its hollow fangs. Of course, the scientist has to be careful not to get bitten in the process.

Venom from the deathstalker scorpion is being used to help people too. Scientists found a protein in scorpion venom that can cross the blood-brain barrier (BBB). The BBB is like a gate. It lets helpful chemicals from the bloodstream enter the brain. But it stops harmful ones. Scientists also found that once in the brain, the venom protein attaches to cancer cells.

Doctors are studying ways to use this protein to treat brain cancer. In the laboratory, scientists attach a **radioactive** element to the protein. Radioactive proteins are injected into a patient. As the proteins travel through the BBB, they attach to cancer cells. Then the radioactive element kills the cancer. Scientists believe this targeted therapy could be more effective than current cancer treatments because it doesn't kill healthy cells.

radioactive: made up of atoms that give off radiation

Brain

1

2

3

4

5

1 Blood rushes through the blood vessel.

2 Vessel walls in the brain form a tight gate called the blood-brain barrier.

3 Toxins and bacteria are not allowed past the BBB.

4 Oxygen, water, and sugars pass through the BBB into the brain.

5 Radioactive venom protein passes through the BBB into the brain.

FEELS LIKE CHICKEN

Maybe you don't want your doctor giving you a shot of venom. Would you prefer a shot of liquid made from a chicken's head?

Many people suffer from a painful condition called osteoarthritis (OA) of the knee. OA causes knee cartilage to break down. Without cartilage, the bones rub against each other. To help these patients, doctors inject a fluid called hyaluronan (hi-AL-yer-ah-nan) into the knee joint. Like cartilage, this fluid lets the bones glide past one another.

Hyaluronan isn't made in a laboratory. It actually comes from rooster combs. Yes, those red things on chicken heads. All chickens have hyaluronan in their combs, but roosters have the most.

Doctors inject hyaluronan into the knee joint to form a cushion between the bones.

After the roosters are killed for food, their combs are cut off and frozen. At a manufacturing plant, the combs are thawed and sliced into chips. Water is then poured over them. The hyaluronan seeps out of the chips and mixes with the water. Later, the water and hyaluronan mixture is dried into a powder. The powder is used to make a gel-like fluid that is injected into someone's knee.

POOP TRANSPLANT

Here's a procedure that makes maggots look like fun. It's called a stool transplant. And yes, stool is just a nice word for poo.

Your intestines are home to about 500 types of bacteria. Most of these bacteria help you digest your food. You couldn't live without them. But some bacteria are harmful if they grow out of control. When your bacterial balance gets out of whack, issues like severe diarrhea crop up. If antibiotics can't control the bacteria, doctors have to take drastic action.

Doctors need to get helpful bacteria back into the sick person's gut. To do this, they put poop from a healthy person into the sick person. First, they mix healthy poop with salt water. This mixture is spun in a blender and filtered through a coffee filter. Doctors then pour the poopy brew into a tube that leads to the person's stomach. From there, the heathy bacteria make their way to the person's intestines and grow. Back to bacterial balance!

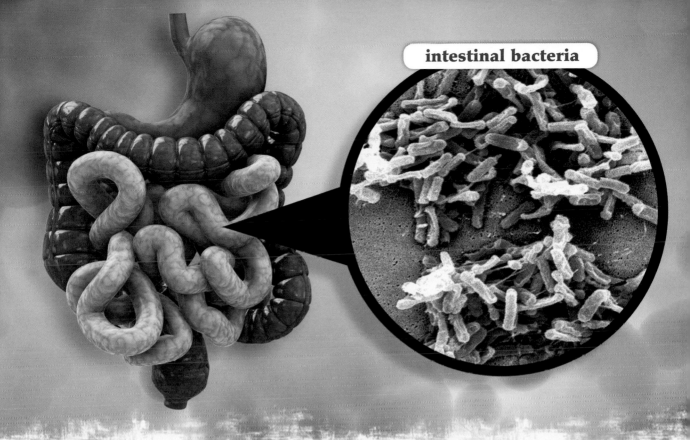

intestinal bacteria

A WARM GLASS OF PEE?

Having someone else's poop in you is bad enough. But what about drinking pee? Some people think drinking urine can be good for you. They believe that pee can treat many conditions including headaches, asthma, and even cancer. Urine often contains vitamins and proteins the body can use. But it also contains waste materials that can be unhealthy. There are no scientific studies that prove drinking pee can help any kind of medical condition.

BANKING ON BLOOD

The human body needs blood to bring oxygen and fuel to cells. Without blood, the body dies. When people lose too much blood, doctors need to put more blood in them. Like a poop transplant, doctors can put another person's blood into you. This procedure is called a blood transfusion.

Where do doctors get the blood for transfusions? It is donated by other people. Most adults have about 10 to 12 pints (5 to 6 liters) of blood in their bodies. When people donate blood, they give up a little less than a pint (.5 liter).

During a blood transfusion, doctors poke a needle into the patient's vein. The needle is connected to a small tube called an IV line. Blood flows through the IV line into the patient's body.

Doctors can't put just any blood into a patient. They must match patients to one of eight different blood types. Some blood types can mix with other types. But others cannot. If the wrong type is used, the two types of blood will clump together. The clumps could cause the patient to die.

FOUL FACT

Diseases can be passed from one person to another through blood transfusions. Doctors are careful to make sure donated blood is safe before it gets used.

GROSS BUT GOOD

So there you have it—bloodsucking worms, snake venom, and rooster heads. These procedures may sound strange, but this medicine works.

And researchers continue to look for amazing ways to save people's lives. Snake venoms contain hundreds of proteins and maybe even thousands of medicines. Right now, scientists are experimenting with a mixture of spider silk and a glasslike compound called silica. This mixture regrows human bones. Maybe someday scientists will find that earwax has amazing healing powers. Who knows what other amazing medical wonders are out there. The ideas may be nasty, but they just might save your life.

-250

GLOSSARY

antibiotic (an-ti-bye-OT-ik)—a drug that kills bacteria and is used to cure infections and disease

blood pressure (BLUHD PRE-shuhr)—the force of blood as it flows through a person's body

blood vessel (BLUHD VESS-uhl)—a tube that carries blood through your body; arteries and veins are blood vessels

enzyme (EN-zime)—a protein in the bodies of humans and animals that causes chemical reactions to occur

flesh (FLESH)—the soft part of a person or animal's body that covers the bones

microorganism (mye-kro-OR-gan-iz-um)—a living thing too small to be seen without a microscope

protein (PROH-teen)—a naturally occurring substance in the body

radioactive (ray-dee-oh-AK-tiv)—made up of atoms whose nuclei break down and give off radiation

stroke (STROHK)—a medical condition caused by a sudden lack of oxygen to the brain; a stroke can cause loss of memory, speech, and strength

tissue (TISH-yoo)—a mass of cells that form a certain part or organ of a person, animal, or plant

READ MORE

Boudreau, Hélène. *Miraculous Medicines*. Science Solves It! New York: Crabtree Publishing, 2009.

Gary, Jeffrey. *Medical Breakthroughs*. Graphic Discoveries. New York: Rosen Central, 2008.

Goldsmith, Connie. *Cutting-Edge Medicine*. Cool Science. Minneapolis: Lerner Publications Co., 2008.

Rooney, Anne. *Health and Medicine: The Impact of Science and Technology*. Pros and Cons. Pleasantville, N.Y: Gareth Stevens Publishers, 2010.

INTERNET SITES

FactHound offers a safe, fun way to find Internet sites related to this book. All of the sites on FactHound have been researched by our staff.

Here's all you do:

Visit *www.facthound.com*

FactHound will fetch the best sites for you!

INDEX